The Classical Piano
Sheet Music Series

INTERMEDIATE
BAROQUE ERA
FAVORITES

ISBN 978-1-5400-8902-1

Visit Hal Leonard Online at
www.halleonard.com

Contact us:
Hal Leonard
7777 West Bluemound Road
Milwaukee, WI 53213
Email: info@halleonard.com

In Europe, contact:
Hal Leonard Europe Limited
42 Wigmore Street
Marylebone, London, W1U 2RN
Email: info@halleonardeurope.com

In Australia, contact:
Hal Leonard Australia Pty. Ltd.
4 Lentara Court
Cheltenham, Victoria, 3192 Australia
Email: info@halleonard.com.au

Contents

Minuet in C minor
BWV Appendix 121

Anonymous

Minuet in D minor
BWV Appendix 132

Anonymous

*These slurs appear in the source manuscript. Other slurs are editorial sugestions.
Tempo, articulations and dynamics are editorial suggestions.

Minuet in G Major
BWV Appendix 116

Anonymous

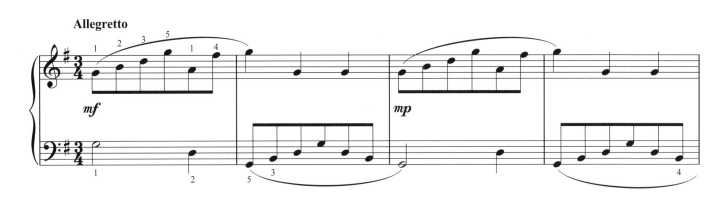

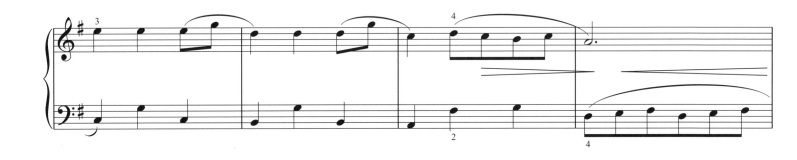

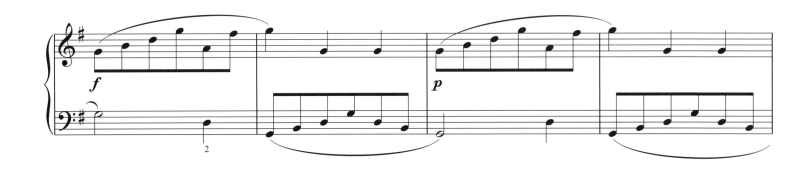

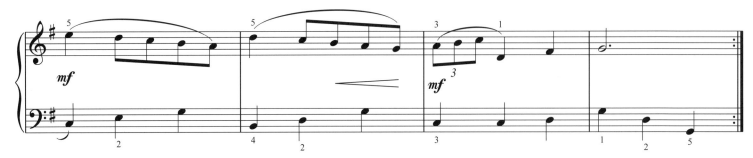

Fingerings, tempo, articulations, and dynamics are editorial suggestions.

Musette in D Major
BWV Appendix 126

Anonymous

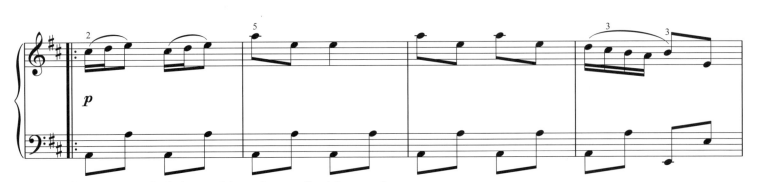

Fingerings, tempo, articulations and dynamics are editorial suggestions.

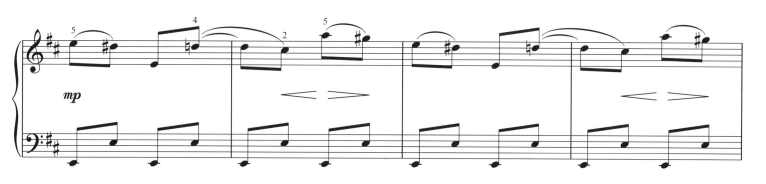

March in D Major
BWV Appendix 122

attributed to Carl Philipp Emanuel Bach
(1714–1788)

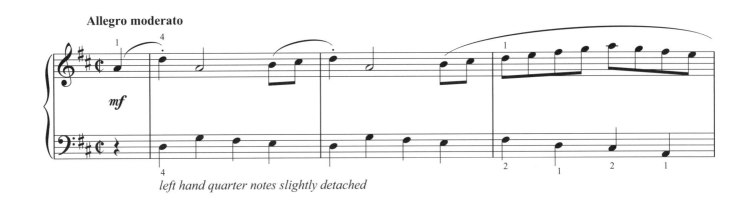

left hand quarter notes slightly detached

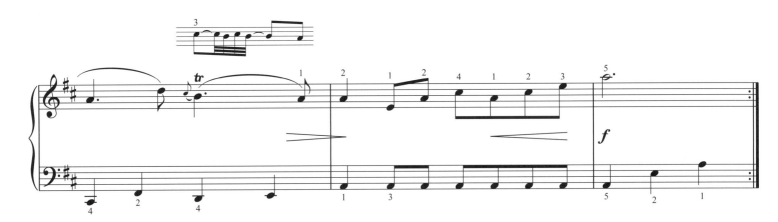

Tempo, articulations and dynamics are editorial suggestions.

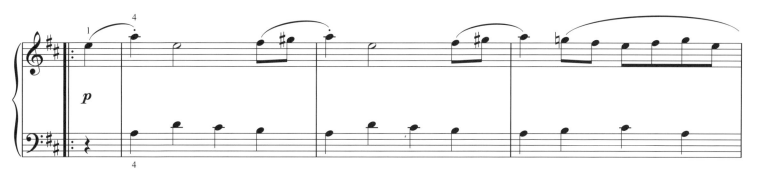

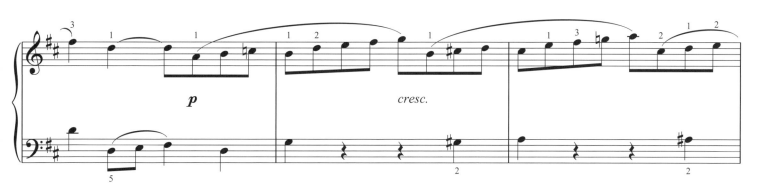

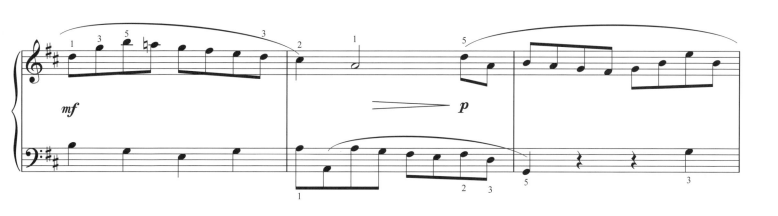

March in G Major

from *The Notebook for Anna Magdalena Bach*, BWV Appendix 124

Carl Philipp Emanuel Bach
(1714–1788)

Tempo, articulations, and dynamics are editorial suggestions.

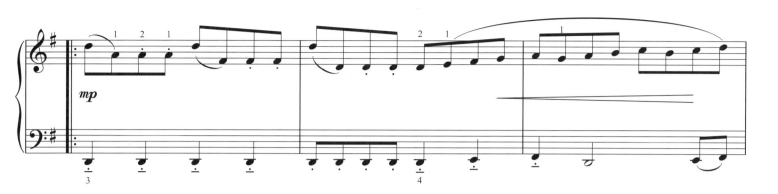

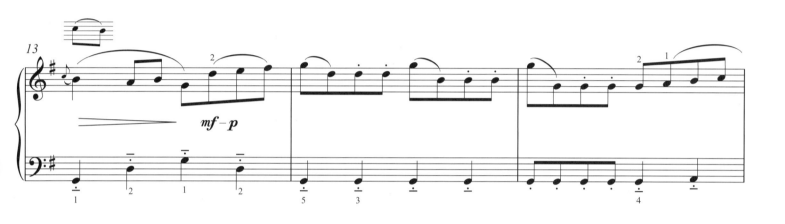

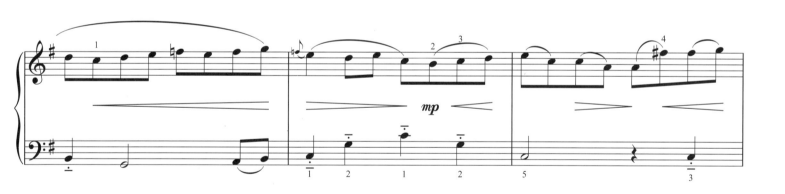

This page has intentionally been left black to facilitate page turns

Solfeggietto in C minor
H. 220

Carl Philipp Emanuel Bach
(1714–1788)

Fingerings and dynamics are editorial suggestions.

left hand over right hand

Invention No. 1 in C Major
BWV 772

Johann Sebastian Bach
(1685–1750)

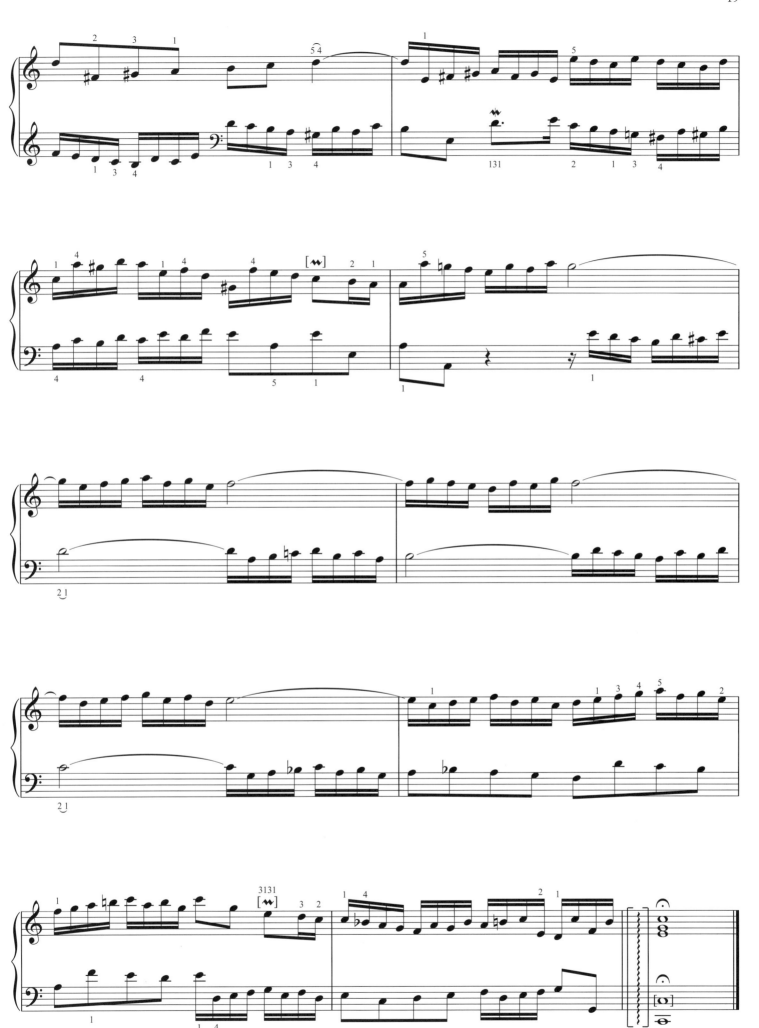

Invention No. 2 in C minor
BWV 773

Johann Sebastian Bach
(1685–1750)

Invention No. 4 in D minor
BWV 775

Johann Sebastian Bach
(1685–1750)

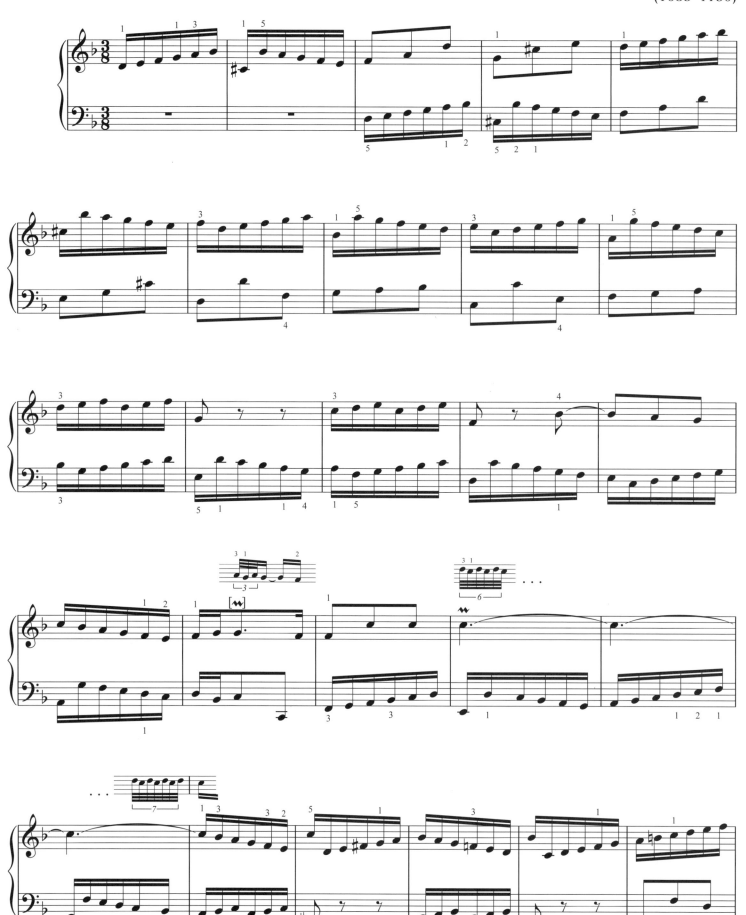

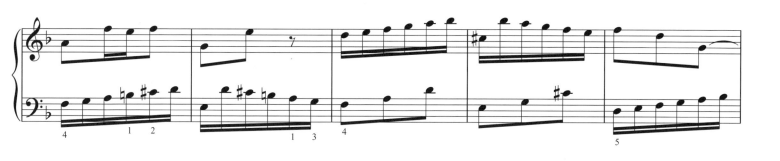

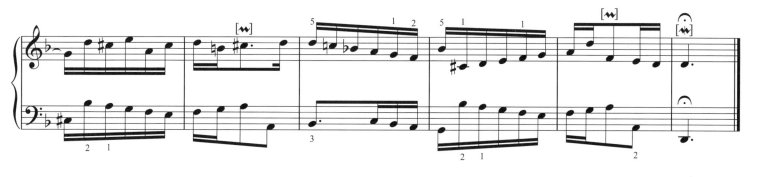

Prelude in C Major

from *The Well-Tempered Clavier*, Book I, BWV 846

Johann Sebastian Bach
(1685–1750)

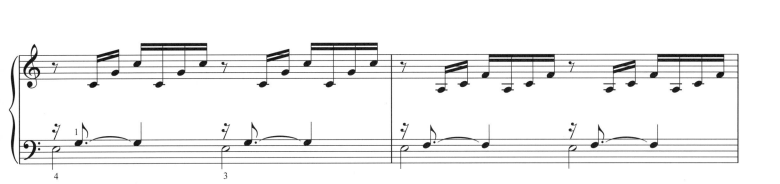

This page has intentionally been left black to facilitate page turns

Prelude in C Major
BWV 924

Johann Sebastian Bach
(1685–1750)

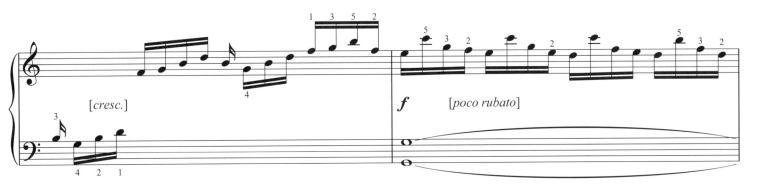

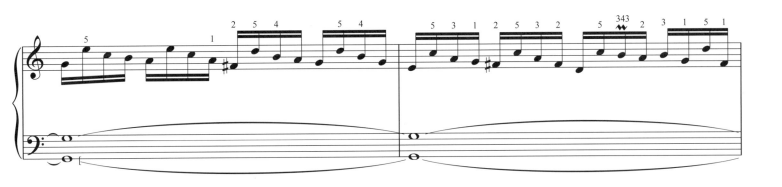

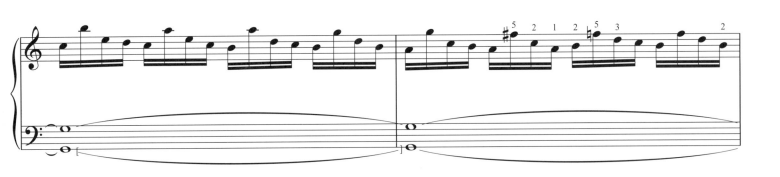

Prelude in C Major
BWV 939

Johann Sebastian Bach
(1685–1750)

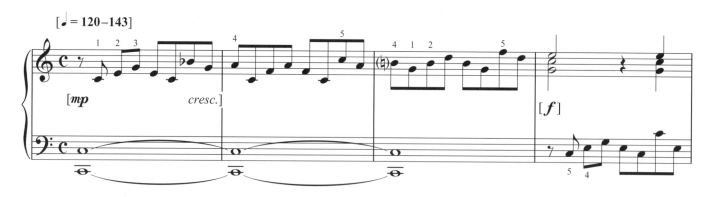

Prelude in C minor
BWV 999

Johann Sebastian Bach
(1685–1750)

[Allegro moderato]

Fingerings are editorial suggestions.

Prelude in D minor
BWV 926

Johann Sebastian Bach
(1685–1750)

Fingerings are editorial suggestions.

Allegro in A Major

Wilhelm Friedemann Bach
(1710–1784)

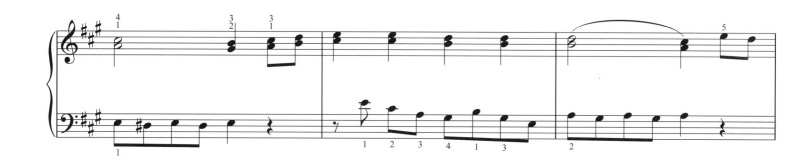

Fine

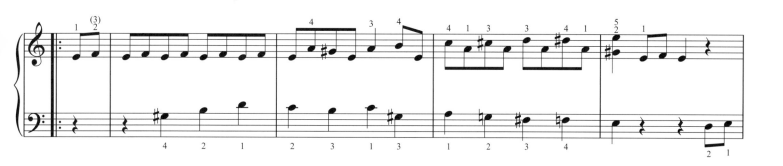

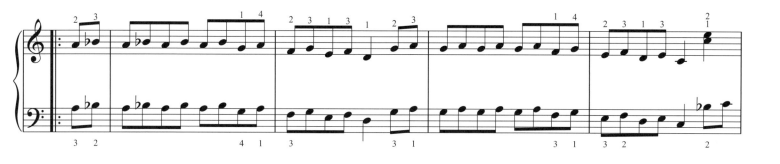

D.C. al Fine

Courante in C Major

John Blow
(1649–1708)

Tempo, dynamics, and articulations are stylistic editorial suggestions. Trills begin on the note above.

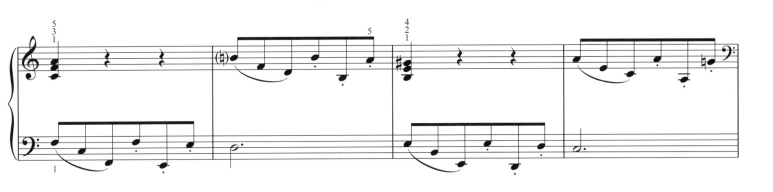

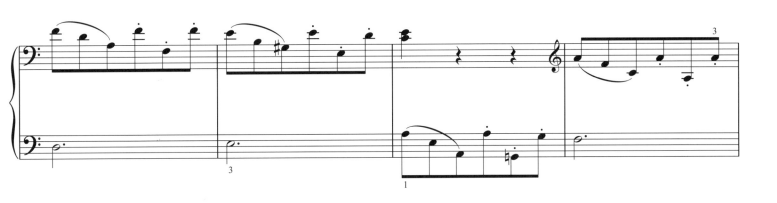

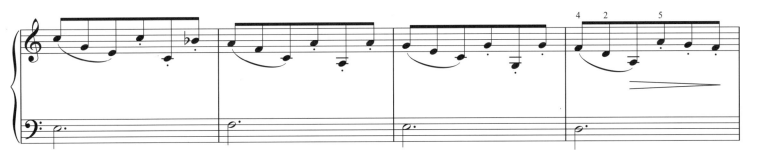

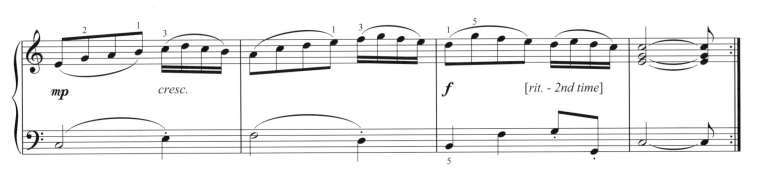

Prelude in C Major

John Blow
(1649–1708)

left hand quarter notes and half notes slightly detached

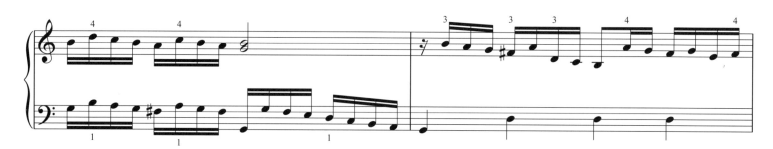

Tempo and dynamics are stylistic editorial suggestions. Trills begin on the note above.

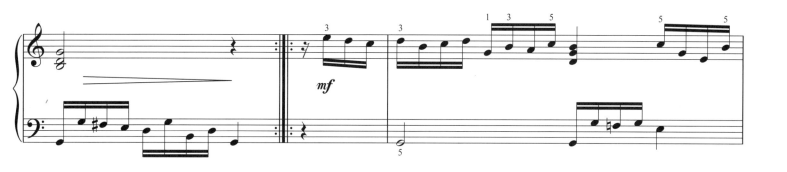

Gavotta in F Major

Arcangelo Corelli
(1653–1713)

Moderato

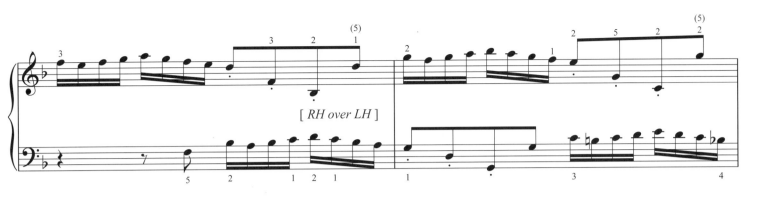

[RH over LH]

This page has intentionally been left black to facilitate page turns

Benevolent Cuckoos Under Yellow Dominos

from *French Follies, or Costumes at a Masked Ball*
from the thirteenth order of Harpsichord Pieces, Book 1

François Couperin
(1668–1733)

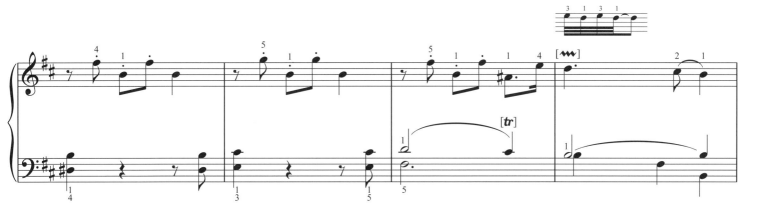

Originally in $\frac{3}{8}$. Tempo, articulation and dynamics are stylistic editorial suggestions. Trills begin on the note above.

Berceuse
(Les graces-naturéles)
from the eleventh order of Harpsichord Pieces, Book 2

François Couperin
(1668–1733)

Tempo, articulations and dynamics are stylistic editorial suggestions. Trills begin on the note above.

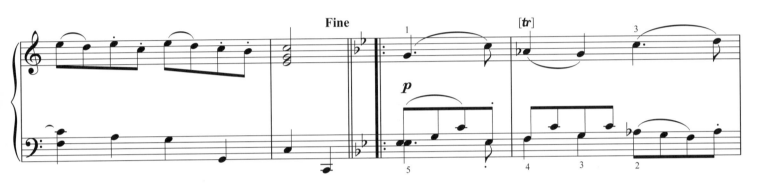

Lament
(La Gémissante)
from the Second Suite of Harpsichord Pieces, Book 1

Jean-François Dandrieu
(c. 1682–1739)

The ornamentation for this piece has been omitted for this edition. Tempo, dynamics and articulations are stylistic editorial suggestions. Trills begin on the note above. Repeat of the first section is optional in performance.

This page has intentionally been left black to facilitate page turns

The Cuckoo
(Le Coucou)
from Harpsichord Pieces, Book 3

Louis-Claude Daquin
(1694–1772)

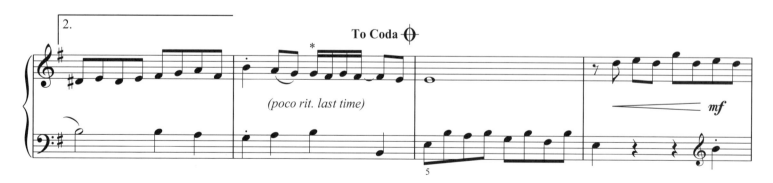

Articulations and dynamics are stylistic editorial suggestions. Ornamentation has been notated for this edition in places marked with *. The original notation was in 2/4, changed in this edition to 2/2.

D.C. al Coda
(with repeat)

CODA

Courante in G Major

George Frideric Handel
(1685–1759)

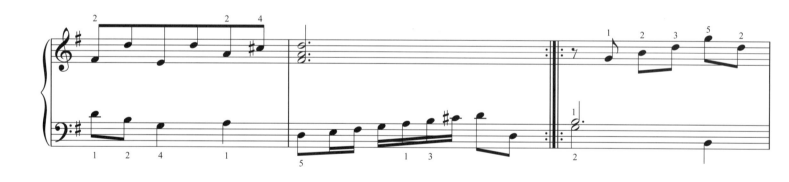

Rigaudon in G Major

George Frideric Handel
(1685–1759)

Tempo, articulations, and dynamics are stylistic editorial suggestions. Trills begin on the note above.

Minuet in F Major

George Frideric Handel
(1685–1759)

Tempo, articulations and dynamics are stylistic editorial suggestions. Trills begin on the note above.

This page has intentionally been left black to facilitate page turns

Sarabande
from Suite in D minor, HWV 437

George Frideric Handel
(1685–1759)

Larghetto

Tempo, articulations, and dynamics are editorial suggestions.

VAR. 1

VAR. 2

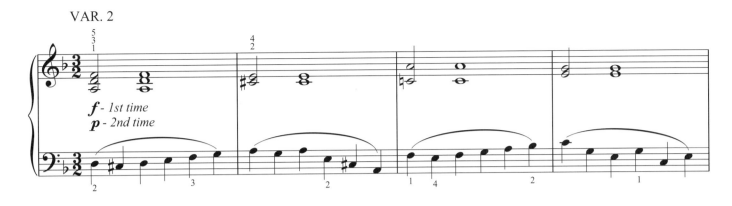

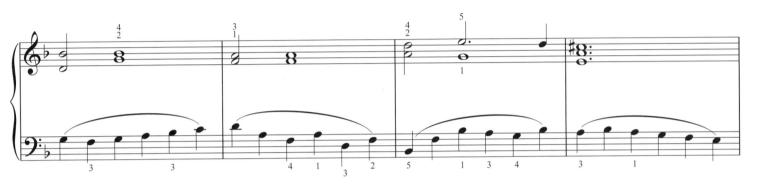

Dance in G Major

Georg Philipp Telemann
(1681–1767)

Sarabande in B-flat Major

Johann Pachelbel
(1653–1706)

Tempo, articulations, and dynamics are stylistic editorial suggestions.

Minuet in G Major
BWV Appendix 114

attributed to Christian Petzold
(1677–1733)

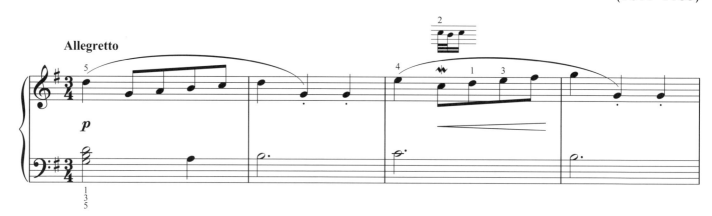

Tempo, articulations and dynamics are editorial suggestions.

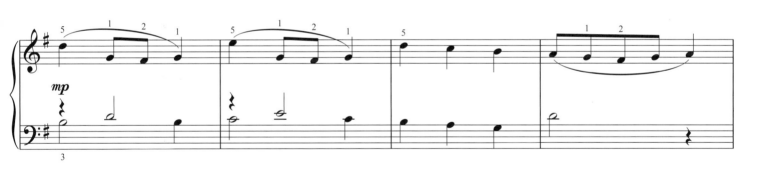

Minuet in G minor
BWV Appendix 115

attributed to Christian Petzold
(1677–1733)

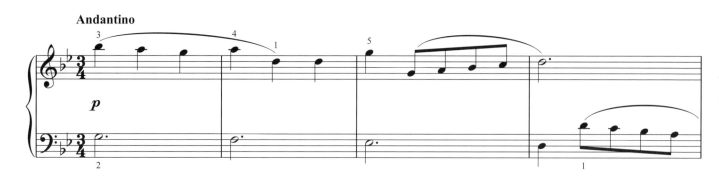

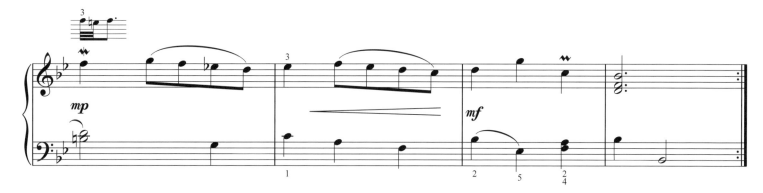

Tempo, articulations and dynamics are editorial suggestions.

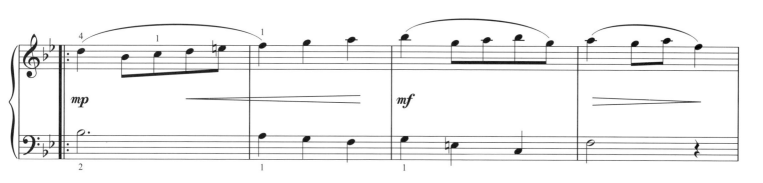

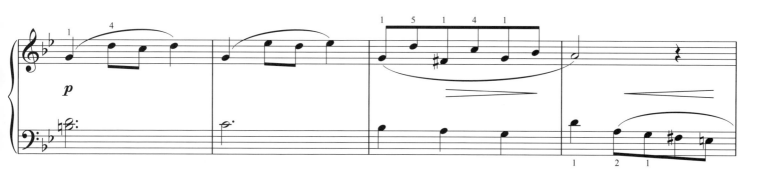

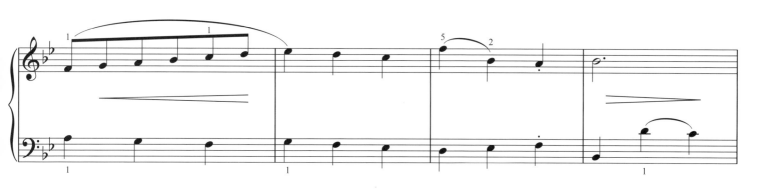

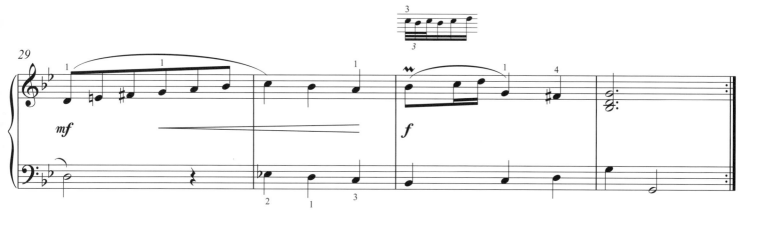

Suite No. 1 in G Major

Henry Purcell
(1659–1695)

Prelude

Allemande

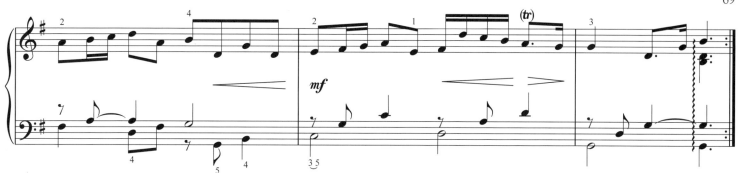

Courante

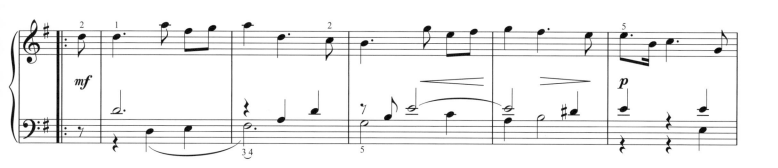

Minuet

Tambourin
from *Pièces de clavecin*

Jean-Philippe Rameau
(1683–1764)

Tempo, articulation and dynamics are stylistic editorial suggestions. Trills begin on the note above.

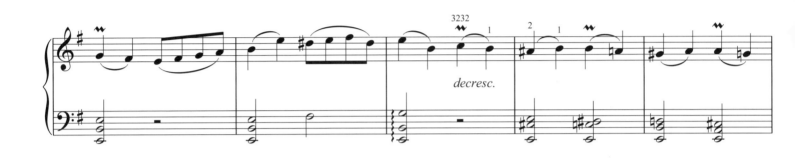

Aria in D minor

Alessandro Scarlatti
(1685–1757)

Articulations and dynamics are stylistic editorial suggestions. Suggested ornamentation has been notated in measures 9–16, 28–33. Trills begin on the note above.

Sonata in A Major
L. 483 (K. 322, P. 360)

Domenico Scarlatti
(1685–1757)

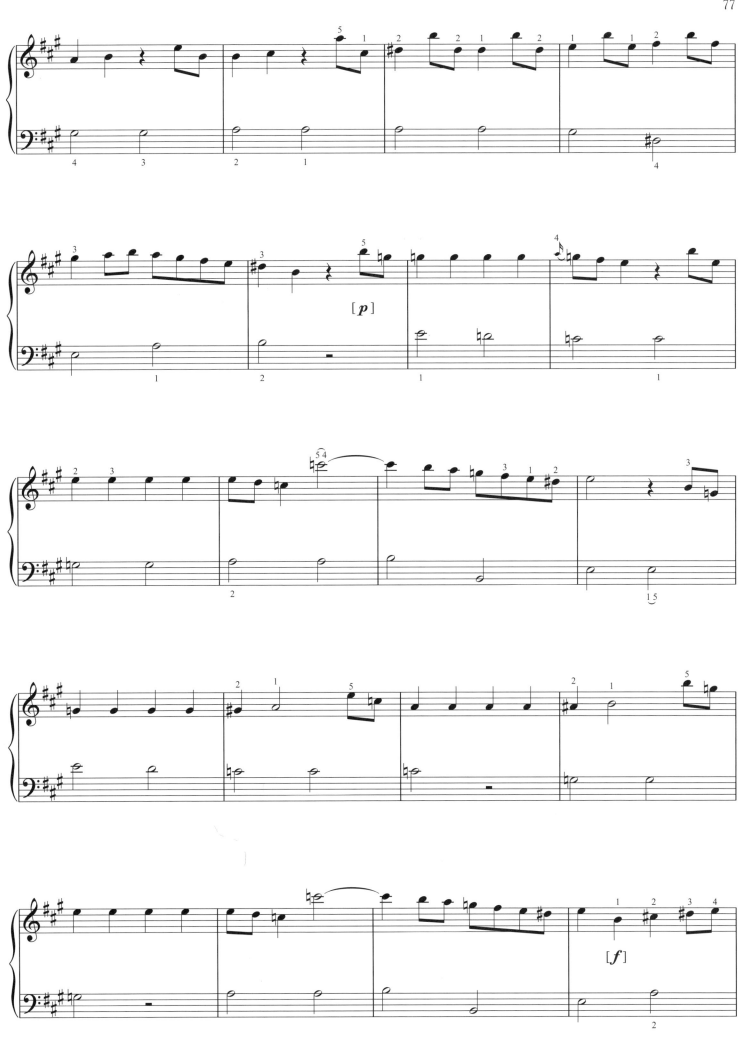

Sonata in A minor
L. 378 (K. 3)

Domenico Scarlatti
(1685–1757)

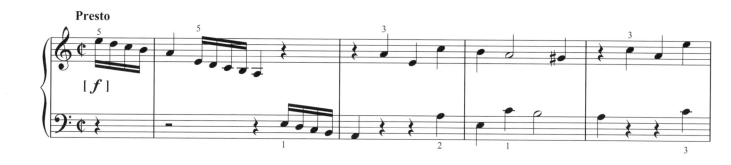

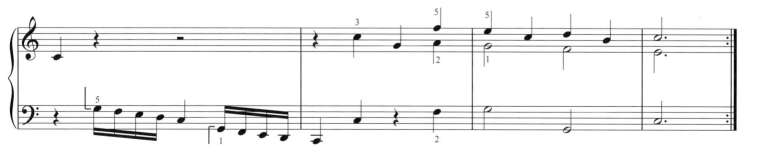

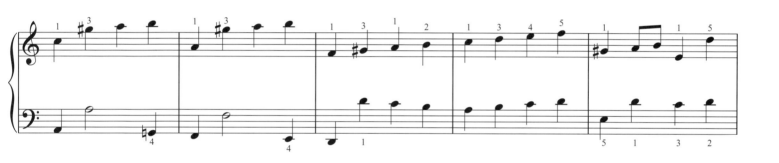

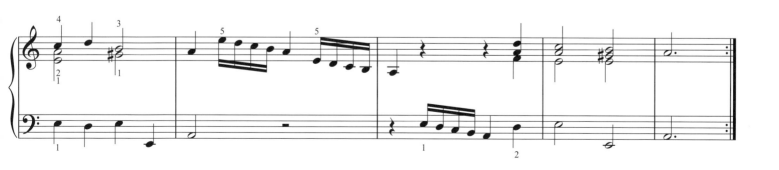

Minuet
from Sonata in C Major, L. 217 (K. 73b, P. 80)

Domenico Scarlatti
(1685–1757)

Fingerings, tempo, articulations, and dynamics are editorial suggestions.
Trills begin on the note above.

Sonata in D minor
L. 423 (K. 32, P. 14)

Domenico Scarlatti
(1685–1757)

Fingerings, tempo, articulations, and dynamics are editorial suggestions.
Ornaments have been realized for this edition.

Sonata in G Major
L. 79 (K. 391, P. 364)

Domenico Scarlatti
(1685–1757)

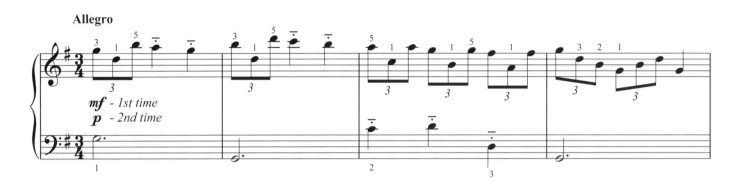

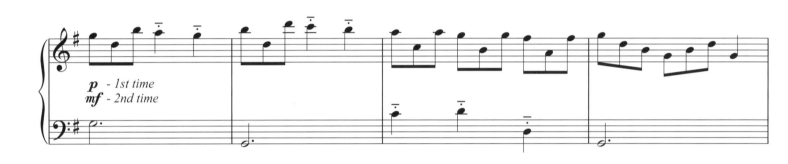

Articulation and dynamics are stylistic editorial suggestions. Trills begin on the note above.